Helia Coelho Mello

Rhetoric

The art of revealing discourse

ScienciaScripts

Imprint

Any brand names and product names mentioned in this book are subject to trademark, brand or patent protection and are trademarks or registered trademarks of their respective holders. The use of brand names, product names, common names, trade names, product descriptions etc. even without a particular marking in this work is in no way to be construed to mean that such names may be regarded as unrestricted in respect of trademark and brand protection legislation and could thus be used by anyone.

Cover image: www.ingimage.com

This book is a translation from the original published under ISBN 978-620-2-03094-6.

Publisher:
Sciencia Scripts
is a trademark of
Dodo Books Indian Ocean Ltd. and OmniScriptum S.R.L publishing group

120 High Road, East Finchley, London, N2 9ED, United Kingdom
Str. Armeneasca 28/1, office 1, Chisinau MD-2012, Republic of Moldova, Europe

ISBN: 978-620-8-34842-7

Copyright © Helia Coelho Mello
Copyright © 2024 Dodo Books Indian Ocean Ltd. and OmniScriptum S.R.L publishing group

SUMMARY

Chapter 1   **2**
Chapter 2   **16**
Chapter 3   **40**

I RHETORIC UNMASKS DISCOURSE[1]

1. READING

Reading is first and foremost about understanding discourse and, in order to understand an argumentative text, the reader needs to identify, in the construction of the writing, the way in which the author presents the arguments in defense of his convictions. Simply deciphering words is a long way from understanding.

It is from this perspective that we consider knowledge of argumentative techniques and rhetorical resources to be a promising way of promoting reading comprehension. In this practice, the study of Rhetoric can be an efficient way of making subjects well prepared to understand an argumentative text.

We consider Rhetoric to be the "mother" of discourse studies and, with so many years of life, it has certainly generated and will continue to generate "daughters". For this reason, whenever necessary and convenient, we have sought knowledge from some of these "daughters", theoretical sources that we believe are related to our purpose, such as Argumentative Semantics and Stylistics, trying to make a connection between the concepts presented by these and those presented by Rhetoric and which have guided our analysis: audience, types of arguments and rhetorical resources used in persuasion.

2. RHETORIC: YESTERDAY AND TODAY

For common sense, Rhetoric is synonymous with artificiality, falsehood or pompous speech. Few people think of Rhetoric as being associated with communicative discourse, argumentation and persuasion, its primary purpose.

Rhetoric can currently be defined (HALLIDAY, 1999, p.8-9) as "the use of communication to define things in the way we want others to see them" or as "a discipline or subfield within human communication studies. It is concerned with examining, describing, prescribing and evaluating acts and events aimed at influencing

---

[1] Article on the paper entitled "Rhetoric unmasks discourse: Knowledge of argumentative techniques and rhetorical resources in the process of reading argumentative texts", presented by the author at the inaugural edition of the International Congress of Critical Applied Linguistics (ICCAL), held in Brasilia, DF, Brazil, from October 19 to 21, 2015.

perceptions, feelings, attitudes and actions with words and other symbols".

In classical civilizations, Rhetoric encompassed both the art of speaking well (eloquence) and the study of persuasion techniques. Thus, from the outset, it took on a pragmatic character: convincing the interlocutor of the truth of your speech, appearing as the art (technique) of persuasion by word of mouth. The Sophists, masters of the art of speaking well, were the first teachers who taught the art of politics and the qualities indispensable for the formation of good citizens, which included Rhetoric, or "the art of persuasion" practiced in courts and other assemblies. However, it was with Aristotle that Rhetoric was transformed into a "science" - that is, a body of knowledge, categories and rules - which those who wish to speak well and convince must apply in their discourse, conceiving it as a rigorous technique of argumentation and as an art of style.

Greek and Roman rhetoric broadly maintained these lines of Aristotle's Rhetoric until the Middle Ages. From the 1st century BC, also during the Roman Empire, Rhetoric enjoyed great prestige. Many of the most famous Roman orators - including Cicero and Quintilian - wrote important works on Rhetoric.

Souza (1999, p.7) states that

Cicero (II-I BC) developed the practice of Aristotelian rhetoric and supported the inter-complementary nature of rhetoric and philosophy: the anonymously-authored treatise *Rhetorica ad Herennium* (cc.I BC) disseminated and popularized Greek sources, establishing rhetorical terminology in Latin; Quintilian (cc.I-II AD) established the pedagogy of Aristotelian rhetoric.

But then, for a long time, Rhetoric was relegated to the level of a mere mundane practice made up of stylistic artifices.

Barthes (1975 apud SOUZA, 1999, p.8-9), states:

In a process that dragged on until the 19th century (the century that marked its demise), Rhetoric gradually lost influence and reduced its field, undergoing the following changes: it lost its immediate pragmatic objective, moving from teaching how to persuade to teaching how to make "beautiful speeches" and limiting itself, from the 16th to the 19th centuries, to the treatment of "figures".

This trend was aggravated by the predominance of Cartesian - positivist thinking in Western philosophy and sciences. The decline of rhetoric began at the end of the 16th century and was due to the rise of bourgeois thinking, which favored the criterion of evidence. Reboul (1998, p.81) points to two other new currents of thought that led to the decline of Rhetoric: "positivism, which rejects rhetoric in the name of scientific truth" and "Romanticism, which rejects rhetoric in the name of sincerity".

For these reasons, "the study of the means of proof used to obtain adherence has been completely neglected (...) by logicians and theorists of knowledge" (PERELMAN, 1999, p.53). This orientation is explained by the fact that argumentation only occurs when there is doubt about a certain thesis, there is no point in arguing about the obvious. Rhetoric is not concerned with what is certain, evident, but with problems whose solution cannot be provided only by experience, by logical deduction; its domain is also that of the verisimilar, the plausible, the probable.

Thus, for a long time, Rhetoric was stripped of its rational "status" and relegated to the level of a mere mundane practice made up of stylistic artifices. From the Middle Ages to the 20th century, there were classic resurgences of Rhetoric (such as those that took place during the Renaissance and the Enlightenment) which, however, did not lead to the recovery of its intellectual dignity (REBOUL, 1998, p.79-82).

It wasn't until the middle of the 20th century that rhetoric began to be rehabilitated.

In the 1960s (20th century), the MU group, Gerard Genette, Henri Morrier, Jean Cohen and Roland Barthes, studied rhetoric as a study of the style of figures whose aim was to make the text poetic, but only as "knowledge of the language procedures characteristic of literature (...) This 'new rhetoric' is therefore limited to elocution, and of this only the figures. In short, rhetoric without any purpose". (ibid, p. 88)

This literary rhetoric is opposed by Chaim Perelman and Lucie Olbrechts-Tyteca, who approached Rhetoric as argumentation and human coexistence, presenting argumentative techniques and emphasizing the need to observe the "audience" that will be the recipient of our speech in order to make the necessary adaptations so that our language fulfills its role: that of persuasion. In his 1958 work - Treatise on Argument - written in partnership with Lucie Olbrechts-Tyteca, Perelman presented a new theory to explain the practical reasoning of speakers, which he called the "New Rhetoric". According to Reboul (ibid, p. 88), "this work, which is part of the great rhetorical tradition of Aristotle, Isocrates and Quintilian, is really the theory of persuasive discourse". In it, Perelman emphasizes the importance of knowing the different types of arguments so that the speaker can use them appropriately in each situation. Investigating how a speaker achieves the acceptance of an audience, a term he uses to define the group of people whom he wishes to influence by his argument, became a particular interest for the author. Argumentation only makes sense if contact is established between the minds of the speaker and his audience; "every speech is addressed to an audience" (PERELMAN, 1999, p.7). If the enunciator knows the audience well, he can induce them to agree with the thesis proposed, presenting in examples, illustrations, analogies and models, beliefs and values that they know, are interested in and accept.

By presenting various argumentative schemes in his work, Perelman offers the reader a sufficient theoretical basis to choose the possible interpretations based on the analysis of the arguments used by the author in order to persuade his audience, establishing communion with them and creating a presence.

However, by presenting a typology of argumentative schemes in his work, he reduced the space for figures. Reboul (1998, p. 89) comments on this "flaw" in Perelman's new rhetoric, saying that "it is a rhetoric centered on invention rather than elocution (...). While the treatise wonderfully describes the strategies of argumentation, it fails to recognize the affective aspects of Rhetoric, the *delectare* and the *movere*, the charm and the emotion, essential, however, to persuasion".

3. RHETORIC AND READING

In order to construct a text, you must first know how to *read*. Those who know how to read argumentative texts, observing and understanding the use of argumentative techniques and rhetorical resources used by an author, will find it easier to produce their own texts and be better able to persuade others of their ideas. They will be able to move beyond the superficial level of reading and reach a deeper understanding of the text.

If Rhetoric is the art of good argument, the art of the word; and reading, among other definitions, is the art of reading and therefore understanding a text; it is necessary to emphasize the importance of Rhetoric and the close relationship it has with reading.

Reboul (ibid, p.139) states that "rhetorical reading is a dialog". Faced with a text, the reader asks "who is speaking?", "when?", "why?" and, above all, "how?" and "to whom?". By answering to whom one is speaking, one defines the audience one wants to persuade; and by analyzing how one speaks, the reader understands the purpose of the use of strategies in the text, thus understanding the unity of the discourse, its central motive.

Reboul (ibid.90) states that "it is necessary to deny the deadly opposition between the rhetoric of argument and the rhetoric of style. One is not without the other". While the arguments correspond to the *logos* of the argument, the rhetorical resources seduce the reader for the pleasure of reading *(pathos),* serving to make the argument accepted.

3.1. Arguments

According to Fiorin (2014, p.69)

An argument is a set of propositions designed to make a given thesis accepted. To argue is therefore to construct a discourse that aims to persuade. Like any discourse, an argument is an utterance, resulting from a process of enunciation, which involves three elements: the enunciator, the enunciated and the discourse, or, as the rhetoricians called it, the speaker, the audience and the argument itself, the discourse.

The **example** *is* a particular case that the speaker uses to support his assertion about another previous case, different but of the same genre, because it has certain common characteristics. Arguments based on examples aim to generalize, establishing a general principle based on a specific case or the probability of repetition of identical cases. They serve to prove, to substantiate the rule.

Comparison *is* considered a persuasive strategy because it allows the speaker to present the compared objects according to his preferences and persuasive intentions. Through this resource, the speaker induces the listener to accept his thesis. It consists of confronting two truths and concluding on the relationship between them. Pauliukonis (1996, p.48) states that "in order to know the relationship between two things, *it is* necessary to know the two parts beforehand", and that "comparisons are made by subjective criteria and confrontation is the instrument that language uses to define individuality". Because it is subjective, comparison always tends to modify a pre-existing state of affairs and "lends itself much more to serving as an argument in favor of the sender's reasoning, rather than as objective information about the facts of reality" (idem), as well as being a strategy used by the sender to abstract arguments capable of capturing the interlocutor's adherence to their thesis and leading them to an expected conclusion.

Analogical reasoning establishes comparisons between similar situations. In order to formulate analogical reasoning correctly, it is essential that the similarities between the situations are much more relevant, much more important than the differences.

3.2 Rhetorical resources

The use of involvement strategies in written texts helps to promote a more intense interpersonal relationship with the audience you want to persuade. One of the first steps in exerting influence is to create lakes, which is why the appeal to emotion *(pathos)* is very important in argumentative texts.

There are various rhetorical resources that can be observed in these texts: titles, rhetorical figures, argumentative operators, verb tenses, modal indicators, impositions, use of presuppositions, segmentation, lexical selection, ambiguities, polysemy and many others.

In this article, we will focus on the use of **rhetorical figures**, **argumentative operators** and **lexical selection**.

Stylistics is a science that deals with the system of affective language, since it studies linguistic expression in terms of its ability to move and suggest the reader or listener. The processes of style affirmation were already the object of study for Rhetoric in its origins. For this reason, Stylistics is often confused with Rhetoric. Giraud (1978, p.7) says that "stylistics, in its twofold form, is modern rhetoric" and (ibid,p.149) "the aspect of the utterance that results from the choice of means of expression determined by the nature and intentions of the individual who speaks or writes".

Giraud (ibid, p.126) states that there are expressive values that reflect the individual's character, temperament, feelings, desires, social origin and situation. There are also expressive values, such as the aesthetic value of the sounds, figures and syntactic structures used, which represent the speaker's intentions and the impression he wants to produce. According to the author (ibid, p.126), all these compositional devices were already recognized and classified by ancient rhetoric, in the processes of invention and arrangement.

We're interested in looking at **rhetorical figures** in stylistics, since they play an important role in persuasion. Reboul (1998, p.113-114) says that "The figure is only rhetorical when it plays a persuasive role", and, "if the argument is the nail, the figure is the way to nail it". Figures of speech (puns, clauses and derivations) relate to the sound material of a speech and their persuasive power is due to the fact that they facilitate attention and recall. Those of meaning (metonymy, metaphor, hyperbole, paradox), according to Reboul (ibid, p.120), play a "lexical role; not that they add words to the lexicon, but that they enrich the meaning of words". The constructional ones concern the structure of the sentence, sometimes of the discourse. Some are by subtraction (ellipsis, reticence); others by permutation (chiasm) and repetition (antithesis, epanalepsis, epanastrophe, anaphora, pleonasm, gradation). There are also figures of speech and figures of thought. Figures of thought are, for example, allegory and irony. Some figures of speech are: personification; apostrophe; silepsis. Figures of speech also have great persuasive power. Some of them are: prolepsis, rhetorical question, hypotyposis.

Argumentative Semantics is a new line of thinking about language that emerged with Oswald Ducrot and Carlos Vogt. According to Geraldi (2000, p.82), "recourse to the notions of argumentative semantics provides an explanation for facts in which traditional classifications or even more careful semantic analysis prove insufficient". According to the author, there was an interest in analyzing categories that concerned "less the syntax or objective content of sentences, and more their possible use in the interaction of speakers" (ibid, p.81).

Issues such as the study of the meaning of grammatical constructions, implicatures, presuppositions and the use of argumentative operators are typical of the study of this science. **Lexical selection** is also a very important rhetorical resource, as it is used to establish oppositions, word games, metaphors, rhythmic parallelisms, etc. The choice of terms has great argumentative power - both a usual and an unusual term in everyday language can be at the service of argumentation - allowing the use of expressions appropriate to their persuasive objectives in the argumentative text. This choice guides the listener to accept the argumentative discourse and, according to Geraldi & Ilari (2000, p.47), "often reflects a concern to evoke or respect a certain level of speech, a certain type of interaction".

Argumentative operators are elements that are part of the grammar of the language - invariable grammatical classes (adverbs, prepositions, conjunctions, adverbial locutions, prepositives, conjunctives) or words denoting inclusion, exclusion, rectification and considered by it only as linking elements, with no semantic content. According to Maingueneau (1996, p. 63), "the opposite occurs in the study of argumentation, which sees in these functioning elements, as effective as they are discreet, one of the essential mechanisms of language persuasion".

The term "argumentative operators" was introduced by Oswald Ducrot, founder of Argumentative Semantics, to designate certain elements of the grammar of a language whose function is to indicate ("show") the argumentative force of the statements, the sense to which they point. If all the statements point to the same conclusion, they belong to an argumentative class. If two or more statements in a class are presented in a gradation of increasing strength in the direction of the same conclusion, there is an argumentative scale (KOCH, 2000, p.30).

Guimaraes (2001a, p.109-122) states that when using but, the speaker uses the "suspense strategy" and when using although, the speaker uses the "anticipation strategy", announcing that the argument introduced by this conjunction will be annulled. The speaker introduces a possible argument for a certain conclusion and then puts a decisive argument for the conclusion he wants to reach. In doing so, he reinforces his argument, leading the listener to adhere to his thesis.

To illustrate the importance of analyzing arguments and rhetorical resources, an argumentative text will be analyzed below as a suggested reading. The chronicle was chosen because it falls into the category of opinionated journalism which usually expresses a view on a given subject.

4. READING A TEXT COMPREHENSIVELY

THE OWNER OF THE BOOK

Martha Medeiros - Zero Hora - 06/11/11

The other day I read a true story told by the Moçambican writer Mia Couto. He said that he once came home at the end of the day, after dark, when a humble 16-year-old boy was waiting for him, sitting on the wall. The boy was holding one of his arms back, which disturbed the writer, who thought he might be mugged.

But then the boy showed him what he had in his hands: a book by Mia Couto himself. Is this your book? asked the boy. Yes, replied the writer.

I came to return it. The boy explained that a few hours earlier he had been in the street when he saw a girl with that book in her hands, the cover of which had the author's picture on it.

The boy recognized Mia Couto from the pictures he had seen in the newspapers. So he asked the girl: Is this Mia Couto's book? She replied: Yes. The boy quickly snatched the book from her hands and ran to the writer's house to do the good deed of returning the work to its true owner.

A story like this could happen in any country inhabited by people who are not yet familiar with books - including here in Brazil. Whose book is it? The answer is not the same as when you ask: "Who wrote the book?".

The author is the one who writes, but the book belongs to the reader, and this in a much broader sense than the concept of private property - I bought it, it's mine. The book belongs to the reader even if it's been taken out of a library, even if it's been borrowed, even if it's been found on a park bench.

The book belongs to those who have access to its pages and through them can imagine the characters, the settings, the voice and the way they move. It is the reader's feelings, the sadness, the euphoria, the fear, the amazement, everything that is conveyed by the author, but which reflects on the reader in a very personal way. It's the reader's pleasure. The reader identifies. The reader learns. And the reader's book.

A few days ago I recorded a radio commercial for the State Book Institute in which I told readers exactly that: my books are your books. And indeed they are. There is no such thing as a book without a reader. It doesn't exist. It's a phantom object that serves no purpose.

That boy from Mozambique doesn't see it that way. For him, the book belongs to whoever has their name stamped on the cover, as if that were a sign of ownership. He has no idea how the whole process works, he's probably never been in a bookshop, nor does he know what a print run is.

But in his disillusionment, he was kind enough to try to put things right, even if he stole a girl's book without realizing it.

She owned the book. And she must have been stunned. A Mia Couto fan snatched her copy. He didn't take his cell phone or wallet, he just wanted the book. A damn lover of literature, she must have thought. So are the stories written by life, interpreted in their own way by each owner.

This text was first published in the Sunday newspaper Zero Hora on November 6, 2011, in the Donna section. It was later published in O Globo magazine (25/11/2012) and in the book "A Graga da Coisa" (LP&M).

After reading the text, we should ask what thesis was defended, to which audience it was addressed, what arguments and rhetorical resources were used. In this case, the argument was made using inductive reasoning, since the thesis only appears in the fifth paragraph of the text. At first, the chronicler is talking to book readers. She is talking to someone who is used to reading and therefore understands the uniqueness of what her chronicle is trying to convey: the author of the book is also you.

The author makes a creative introduction so that the audience is in communion with the thesis she is going to present in the first paragraph. She recounts an event that happened to the writer Mia Couto, using the first person. He starts from a personal example and then transforms the subject into something broader and of interest to his readership. It is possible to see that, although the process of meaning is constructed from a particular event known to the chronicler, the meaning produced by the text concerns something that happens to most people, or to the average person. This can explain why this text, despite initially being published in a notebook aimed at women, ends up reaching a universal audience. The particular example used in the first three paragraphs leads to a general case since the author says: "a story like this could happen in any country inhabited by people who are not yet familiar with books". The use of the em dash in the fourth paragraph serves to emphasize the statement that follows: "here in Brazil".

She makes it clear to the reader who Mia Couto is through the expression "Moçambican writer". This is a resource often used in argumentation: the clarification of a term without the audience realizing that the author may be considering their ignorance or lack of knowledge of this term; it's a good strategy for reaching a universal audience; even people who don't know current writers will understand what the author of the text is saying about this person quoted in the initial example.

The use of direct speech in the second paragraph is also a rhetorical device because, through it, the reader imagines the situation; this is a rhetorical figure called hypotyposis - we make present, through words, what is absent.

The argumentative operator "inclusive" reinforces the argument presented. Immediately afterwards, the problem that generated the argument is presented: "whose book is it?". And the answer given anticipates a possible question that could be asked by the audience to be persuaded: "who wrote the book?".

Geraldi (2000, p.82) says that "the <u>but</u> thus serves to divert the listener from a more or less expected conclusion, thus altering the argumentative orientation that the speaker gives to the verbal interaction in which he is taking part". The argumentative operator "but" announces the thesis being defended: the book belongs to the reader. To defend this thesis, the author uses the argument by comparison, comparing the concept of ownership of an object with that of ownership of a book.

The use of the argumentative operator "same" reinforces the thesis and the repetition of this operator (anaphora) even more. Moreover, in this passage, there is a gradation: the book belongs to the reader even when it has been "taken out of the library", "borrowed", "found on a plague bank".

In the sixth paragraph, the rhetorical figure called hypotyposis appears again. Through description, the reader of the chronicle is put in the place of the reader of a book. Gradation is also used when talking about the properties of the reader with provoked sensations: "sadness", "euphoria", "fear", "amazement", "everything that is transmitted by the author". And the author emphasizes the property of the reader through anaphora; she repeats "the reader's" several times.

In the following paragraph, a confessional attitude is used to promote "pathos" and build "ethos". Talking about oneself is a way of bringing the reader into communion with the enunciator of the text. By openly confessing to the reader, the enunciator establishes a bond of friendship with him. It's as if he were his intimate friend. This establishes a pact, a communion between minds and makes it easier to achieve the main objective of an argument: persuasion, acceptance of the proposed thesis through an appeal to *pathos,* since the reader is moved by the confessions made to him. Through this emotional appeal, the enunciator's discourse is also given greater credibility (appeal to *ethos)*Through the narration of a fact that happened to her, the author transmits information so that the reader can perceive the credibility of who is speaking to them, her competence to speak about reading so that she can gain the credibility of the audience.

In this same paragraph, anaphora is also present through the repetition of the statement "does not exist". The purpose of the repetition is to emphasize the idea that there is no such thing as a book without a reader, in order to highlight its importance.

Lexical selection was also a great resource; terms like "owner", "possession" serve to reinforce the idea of ownership.

In the final paragraphs of the text, there is a return to the creative introduction made in the first three. This shows that there was a concern with the construction and structure of the text. In the last paragraph, in particular, there is a reinforcement of the thesis through this return to the initial example: everyone appropriates and interprets the stories in their own way, becoming the owners of the books, which doesn't mean owning them. To reinforce this idea, the gradation "cell phone", "wallet", "book" was used. In this way, the term "book" is valued among the other objects.

The author concludes her text by amplifying the meaning of what she said: "book is life" by making an analogy in the last line of her argument.

FINAL CONSIDERATIONS

As we have seen, there are many rhetorical resources and argumentative strategies that can be used in persuasive argumentation. Of course, the task of listing them will always be incomplete, since various resources used in a written text whose aim is to persuade a particular audience can be considered as such.

However, we believe that the approach taken has been sufficient to make the reader of this article aware of the importance of recognizing these when reading a persuasive speech and that they can read it effectively, unmasking its true meaning.

BIBLIOGRAPHICAL REFERENCES

ARISTOTELES. **Rhetoric.** Translated by Edson Bini. Sao Paulo: Edipro, 2011.

Retorica. 2ª ed., revised INCM - Imprensa Nacional- Casa da Moeda, 2005.in Obras Completas de Aristoteles, volume VIII, Tome I, coord. Antonio Pedro Mesquita.

GERALDI, Joao Wanderley & ILARI, Rodolfo. **Semantics.** 10. ed. Sao Paulo: Atica, 2000.

GUIMARAES, Eduardo. **Text and Argumentation: a study of Portuguese conjunctions.** 2. ed. Sao Paulo, Campinas: Pontes, 2001

GIRAUD, Pierre. **A Estilfstica.** 2ª .ed. trad. Miguel Maillet. Sao Paulo: Mestre Jou, 1978.

HALLIDAY, Tereza Lucia. **What is Rhetoric.** Sao Paulo: Brasiliense, 1999 (First Steps Collection: 232).

KOCH, Ingedore G. Villaga. **Argumentation and Language.** 6. ed. Sao Paulo: Cortez, 2000.

MAINGUENEAU, Dominique. **Pragmatics for literary discourse.** Translated by Marina Appenzeller. Marina Appenzeller. Sao Paulo: Martins Fontes, 1996.

MEDEIROS, Martha. The owner of the book. **Zero Hora newspaper.** Porto Alegre, November 11, 2011. Donna section.

PAULIUKONIS, Maria Aparecida Lino. *Comparison and Argumentation. Two complementary notions.* In SANTOS, Leonor Werneck dos (org.) **Discurso, coesao e argumentação.** Rio de Janeiro: Oficina do Autor, 1996, p. 48-56.

PERELMAN, Chaim & OLBRECHTS-TYTECA, Lucie. **Treatise on Argumentation - The New Rhetoric.** Sao Paulo: Martins Fontes, 1999.

REBOUL, Olivier. **Introduction to Rhetoric**. Sao Paulo: Martins Fontes, 1998.

SOUZA, Roberto Aclzelo dos. **The Empire of Eloquence - Rhetoric and Poetry in 19th Century Brazil.** Rio de Janeiro: EdUERJ; EdUFF, 1999.

II- THE RUST-FREE RHETORIC OF GOOD SHINE[2]

1. INITIAL CONSIDERATIONS

"In order for an argument to develop, it really needs those to whom it is addressed to pay some attention to it."

(Perelman:1999, 20)

What makes an advertising campaign successful for so many decades? What is the formula used in the texts to attract the audience?

In this article, we try to answer these questions by analyzing 24 texts printed by Bom Bril on the back covers of magazines in Brazil between 1997 and 2000. Because there were so many advertisements, we chose some texts in which the company's poster boy, Carlos Moreno, represented public figures (Ronaldo, Gil Gomes, Xuxa, Bill Clinton, Walter Mercado, Eneas, Tiazinha, Globeleza, FHC, A Feiticeira, Luciano Huck and Ivete Sangalo, Ratinho, Adriane Galisteu, Ronaldo and Milene, Silvio Santos, Gorete, Joao Gilberto, Sandy and Junior, Ana Maria Braga, Alexandre Pires, Popo, Alberto Roberto, Barrichello, and Nicea Pitta and Pitta) who were known to the housewives of Brazil (the target audience of Bom Bril's advertising campaign).

The ads were selected[3] from the book *Soy Contra Capas de Revistas,* published by the company responsible for creating and disseminating the ads, W/Brasil. In this book, 136 back covers, published from 1997 to 2000, were compiled.

Due to the enormous success of the Bom Bril advertising campaign, not only in our country, but all over the world, we have looked at the reasons that make this campaign such a success and tried to show, through examples of texts, how the use of essentially rhetorical techniques contributes to the belief in a certain truth defended by someone.

There are many rhetorical studies on Bom Bril advertising texts, but many of them focus on verbal and non-verbal language resources and disregard argumentation. Reboul (1998, p.90) states that "it is necessary to deny the deadly opposition between the rhetoric of argument and the rhetoric of style. One is not without the other". For this reason, in this work, in addition to analyzing the rhetorical figures that are essential to provoke passion for persuasive discourse, we use some concepts about Rhetoric that were presented by the philosophers Aristotle and Chaim Perelman, emphasizing the importance of convincing an audience through argumentation.

In Aristotle's work, issues such as rhetorical genres and means of proof (pathos, logos, ethos) will be addressed in this text. Chaim Perelman's theory, presented in *Treatise on Argumentation - The New Rhetoric*, points out issues such as the importance of the audience and communion with the enunciator and a typification of arguments. And through Olivier Reboul, in his book *Introduction to Rhetoric*, we will study the rhetorical figures present in texts.

Our aim in this work is to present Rhetoric, not as a resource for manipulation, but as a technique used by the speaker to convince and persuade an audience through argumentation.

---

[2] Adaptation of the monograph presented for the Specialization course in Rhetoric and Argumentation at the Centro Universitario de Araraquara, Nucleo de Educagao a Distancia, 2015.

[3] Once the back covers of the book had been chosen, the images were found on internet pages for reproduction in this work (attachments), as the publisher does not allow the reproduction of pages from their book.

Advertising discourse is rhetorical par excellence. The advertiser of a consumer product is interested in making a profit by selling his stock and novelties. The potential buyer will always be interested in some kind of comfort, relief, security or pleasure. And if he believes that the advertised product meets his interests, he will be predisposed to buy it. Advertising is about persuading, enticing, inciting to action. To convince, for each case and each type of audience, it uses argumentation.

In Aristotle's work, issues such as rhetorical genres and means of proof *(pathos, logos, ethos)* are addressed in this text.

Of the three rhetorical genres, the judicial, the deliberative and the epideictic, advertising discourse clearly belongs to the last. Several of its characteristics highlight this description. The qualities of things and their characteristics (of consumer goods in advertising) are privileged. Thus, advertising is an epideictic discourse, in the sense that it shows, points out, announces, displays - it makes public, it intends to display its object. The speaker creates communion around certain values recognized by the audience, making use of all the means that Rhetoric has at its disposal to amplify and enhance them. And when there is not enough reason in the product itself to praise it, it is contrasted with the shortcomings and defects of the competition.

The means of proof in advertising also have characteristics presented by Aristotle: in some texts, the speaker lends his credibility to selling the product *(ethos)* and in others there is an appeal to the audience's emotion *(pathos);* rationality (*logos*) does not predominate.

Chaim Perelman's theory, presented in *Treatise on Argumentation - The New Rhetoric*, points out issues such as the importance of the audience and communion with the speaker. Audience is the term used by Perelman to define the group of people whom the speaker wishes to influence by his argument. His concept of audience differs from the Aristotelian one, since in Greece the audience was the group of people physically present around a speaker to listen to his speech. For Perelman, the audience refers to the speaker's or writer's mental conception of the audience. The argument of an oral or written text is always addressed to an audience. According to him (1999, p.7), "the material absence of readers can lead the writer to believe that he is alone in the world, although, in fact, his text is always conditioned, consciously or unconsciously, by those to whom he intends to address it". If there is communion, the speaker will find it easier to persuade others. That's why it's important that the arguments are in agreement with the audience, because only then will there be communion.

Arguments such as comparison and analogy, which were also presented by Perelman, served as the theoretical basis for this work. Comparison and analogy, according to Pauliukonis (1996), are considered efficient strategies because they allow the subject of the discourse to present the compared objects according to his preference and his persuasive intentions. Through this resource, the enunciator induces the listener to accept his opinion. It consists of comparing two truths and concluding on the relationship between them.

And through Olivier Reboul, in his book *Introduction to Rhetoric*, we study the rhetorical figures present in texts (such as puns, metaphors, metonymies, personifications) which play an important role in argumentation. According to Reboul *(ip.cit.,* p.114), "The figure is only rhetorical when it plays a persuasive role", and, "if the argument is the nail, the figure is the way to nail it".

2. THE IMPORTANCE OF RHETORIC

For the ancients, Rhetoric was conceived as a set of principles and rules of communication that had to be taught as part of a thorough education. A young person who was not trained to speak well in public would not be well educated. Thus, the teaching of Rhetoric was basically, but not exclusively, the teaching of oratory techniques. The emphasis of Rhetoric in Antiquity was on the communicator. For the medievals, it was a tool, a purely formal discipline that could be used in various fields of knowledge.

Today, the "New Rhetoric" emphasizes the recipient of the message, commonly referred to as the "public" or "audience[4]" - the reader, the listener, the viewer. Hence the importance of getting to know them in order to use the right rhetorical resources for each situation, using language that they understand and presenting reasons that satisfy them, in short, using a convincing speech as one that makes the audience feel identified with the communicator and their proposal. We act rhetorically when we justify our position in terms acceptable to our audience and identify with their values and interests. Rhetoric is therefore communication that proposes (not imposes) a vision of reality that corresponds to the desires or needs of the sender and the sensibilities and interests of their audience.

2.1 The Rhetoric of a Thousand and One Uses:

Advertising is a rhetorical discourse par excellence. The advertiser of a consumer product is interested in making a profit by selling his stock and novelties. The potential buyer will be interested in some comfort, relief, security or pleasure. And if they believe that the advertised product meets their interests, they will be predisposed to buy it.

The act of persuading in an advertisement doesn't happen by presenting information about what the sender thinks about the product being advertised; it's an elaboration with the aim of transforming the public's point of view, of making an opinion acceptable, when it wouldn't be if it were denied. The advertising text conditions the audience through a number of techniques, influencing their behavior, making them more accessible to the arguments that will be presented to them, seeking to act on the essential tendencies of each person in order to provoke a desire to act in the direction that is favorable to them.

In order to get the individual to take the desired action, the advertising message follows a series of stages corresponding to the various stages of the psychological process. The discourse involves them emotionally, seeks their sympathy, makes them identify with the appeal and want to act in the desired direction.

Rhetoric persuades through discourse. It doesn't resort to violence or an empirical experiment, but seeks the intellectual adherence of the universal audience through the use of argumentation alone. The texts of the Bom Bril advertising campaign emphasize the idea of the product's thousand and one uses, giving the recipient the freedom to choose whether or not to use it.

In order to understand the success and permanence of Bom Bril's advertising text, one must first think of the audience's adherence. Normally, the sales pitch for cleaning products is aimed at housewives and this was also the initial objective of the company's advertisements. However, despite being aimed at a particular audience, the texts of the campaign reached a universal audience[5] - it appealed to the traditional housewife, the one who works outside (but also at home) and at the same time to young people, the literate, the illiterate, the old, men, children, postgraduate students (many academic papers have already been published on the subject), Brazilians and foreigners (awards have been received all over the world). This work analyzes the resources used by Washington Olivetto, the editor of the texts, to achieve this.

---

[4] According to Perelman & Tyteca (1996:22), "the audience is the group of people the speaker wants to influence with his argument". The universal audience, according to Perelman, is the main goal of argumentation.

2.2. The rhetorical genre of advertising, from the point of view of Aristotle and Perelman

Having defined its rhetorical appeal, there remains the question of the genre to which advertising belongs, and the proper places in that genre. Of the three rhetorical genres, judicial, deliberative and epideictic, advertising clearly belongs to the latter.

Several of his characteristics show this description. His discourse is not born out of the immediacy of the debate and confrontation that condition the other two genres (judicial and deliberative); it is prepared in advance by its author and, for this reason, the qualities of things and their characteristics (qualities of consumer goods) are privileged.

Thus, publicity is an epideictic speech (Gr. Epideiktikos, Lat. Demonstratium), in the sense that it shows, points out, announces, displays - it makes public. The speaker creates communion around certain values recognized by the audience, making use of the set of means, of proofs, that Rhetoric has at its disposal to amplify and enhance them.

When discussing the qualities of the proofs used in Rhetoric, Aristotle (2005, p.96-97) states:

We persuade by character when the speech is delivered in such a way that it leaves the impression that the speaker is trustworthy. (...) We persuade by the disposition of the listeners, when they are led to feel emotion through the speech, because the judgments we make vary according to whether we feel sadness or joy, love or hate. (...) Finally, we persuade through discourse, when we show the truth or what seems to be true, based on what is persuasive in each particular case.

Knowing that the main objective of the advertising text is to sell a product, it is also essential to have the notion of the audience revitalized from Aristotle's ideas by the philosopher of the New Rhetoric.

As Perelman *(ip.cit.,* p.27) points out, "the audience has the main role in determining the quality of the argument and the behavior of the speakers".

Perelman's theory sheds light on the communion and presence that must be established between the speaker and the listener. Every speech must be composed with those who will hear or read it in mind. In advertising discourse, the sender must choose the premises that can be accepted by the audience he is addressing and, through his argumentation, convince them to buy the product.

When discussing argumentative techniques, Perelman *(idem,* p.211-465) presents two types of arguments: linking (or associating) and dissociating. The process of association is based on the principle of solidarity. Its aim is to bring elements closer together by establishing a relationship of unity between them. Among these arguments, one can see in the attached texts the use of association arguments, more precisely, arguments that establish the structure of reality: arguments that operate as if by induction, formulating a law, a thesis, establishing generalizations and regularities, proposing models, examples, illustrations based on particular cases or at least the repetition of identical cases to establish what is believed to be a socially constructed structure of reality, through the use of analogies and comparisons.

2.3.. Bom Bril Boy: an auditorium conqueror

For advertising to work, to sell, it must first create a brand image, a positive personality that establishes a "friendly" relationship between the consumer and the product.

The Bom Bril boy, played by actor Carlos Moreno, went down in Brazilian advertising history as a unique case (he's in the *Guinness Book)* for having been the company's poster boy from 1978 to 2004 and then again in 2007, a role he held until 2011. As of April 2007, Moreno had taken part in 337 advertisements as "Garoto Bom Bril"[6] . On April 25, 2013, a new commercial for the company began airing, created by the DPZ agency, in which he returns to the position of Garoto Bom Bril and occupies the brand's bench with comedians Monica Lozzi and Dani Calabresa, members of the campaign entitled "Mulheres Evoluidas" (Evolved Women). He continues to please the public, resisting technological and linguistic changes and fads.

At the beginning, the campaign was designed to advertise the new products manufactured by the Bom Bril company (Brill dishwasher, Limpol detergent and Radium oil) to housewives by associating them with the brand of the famous auger sponge, the company's main product. With no competitors on the market, the Bom Bril sponge, which had been on television since the 1970s, sold millions of units a year.

According to Matos (2007, p.34-35)

In 1978, the Bombril poster boy was "born" with a different and unusual proposal for the times. Cleaning products, which to this day are targeted at women, used to be presented by women in order to create greater public identification with the product. At the time, creating a male character to talk to women about cleaning didn't seem to be very credible. However, Andres Bukowinski, Francesc Petit and Whashington Olivetto dared to change and got it right.

The bubble-blower boy overturned the authoritarian and superior way in which the male sex usually talks to women. Shy, stooped and sympathetic, Carlos Moreno has been talking to housewives with respect and attention ever since. This attitude has earned him the credibility and sympathy not only of housewives, but also of the women and men who also consume Bombril products.

Matos *(idem,* p.51-52) also states:

Until then, commercials for cleaning products were not considered stimulating, from the point of view of advertising creativity, due to the impossibility of varying the theme: explanations of the product's chemical components, imposing technicians evaluating the results, housewives surprised by the product's results, etc.

Realizing that consumers didn't like this type of commercial either, the two directors of DPZ, Francesc Petit and Washington Olivetto, created a campaign that played with the fact. They introduced a very human character, a chemist from the company itself, shy and awkward, embarrassed to be on television, in charge of telling the housewife about the new products he had helped to make. Very polite, he didn't attack competitors, but made it clear that there was always something different about his product. (...)

Played by an actor still unknown to the public, the character had an impact beyond expectations. The campaign, which exposed the fragility of the poster boy at a time when society was full of macho values, was very innovative and was talked about in the press. The Bombril boy represented a new man who was not ashamed to say that he needed to keep his job, with the complicity of the female consumer. As Maria Elisa Albuquerque recalls, "A headline in Propaganda magazine summed it up: 'The commercial that killed the macho'".

The character was given an exceptional shine by Carlos Moreno's performance, earning him a high degree of credibility. His image is perfectly suited to video and

---

[6] The Bombril Boy at http://www.wtennis.com.br/html/revistas/67/carlos.htm Accessed 15/11/2014

magazines and is not imposing. He makes the reader feel more emotionally involved, arousing positive feelings: trust, affection, affinity, joy. It also awakens sympathy for the weak, a characteristic of the personality of many Brazilians. Carlos Moreno himself[7] said that "the image of the coach has been totally diluted. What has always remained is the friendliness, the polite and non-imposing way of putting things across, that more cordial side. I think that's what still creates empathy."

Albuquerque[8] *(apud* Matos: 2007, p. 52) states:

Simplicity was the tone, somewhat reminiscent of those live commercials from the 1950s, when *videotape* was not yet available and the setting of the Bombril films had that touch of improvisation, of being "made up on the spot", like the first advertising girls. The apparent lack of scenographic resources was balanced by extremely verbal scripts, which relied entirely on the actor's interpretation. The huge logo at the back, using strong red and rounded shapes, practically enveloped the poster boy. The advertisement presented a normal person, outside the stereotypes of advertising. He was a commercial anti-hero, whose most powerful weapon was humor. The character was given an exceptional shine by Carlinhos Moreno's performance, earning him a high degree of credibility. It was all very new, very different and, at the same time, very simple. For Washington Olivetto, in a recent interview with the Research Division, "the great merit of this campaign was to treat the housewife as a woman and not as a stove pilot. Her intelligence was more respected".

Albuquerque (1998, p.27-32) states that the public liked him. In the 1981 campaign, created partly to measure the character's effectiveness, three films were made, as if they were chapters in a story. In the first, the Bom Bril Boy, very sad, took off his company apron and said goodbye to the housewife, explaining that he had lost his "little mouth" because of gossip and because people thought he was "a bit like that", subtly hinting at an effeminate manner. In the end, the empty and silent stage left a strong sense of drama in the air. Some of the audience took it seriously and began to jam the company's phone lines, sending letters from all over the country (some threatening to boycott the products if he wasn't hired again). The following month, the second film was aired, showing an unsympathetic replacement who tried to sell the product, but was booed and left in a rage. Shortly afterwards, the last film in the series was broadcast, with the happy Bombril Boy returning to thank "the lady who wrote to the company. Because jobs aren't easy these days".

The character, transposed into a kind of micro-series, moved audiences to such an extent that these commercials broke *recall* records in Sao Paulo and Rio de Janeiro. It was undoubtedly Garoto Bom Bril's most famous and award-winning campaign .[9]

This leads us to believe that in order for an audience to buy in, the speaker needs to win over the audience. This conquest begins with premises accepted by the listener and is mainly emphasized by the artistic means of proof used by the speaker. This contact between the speaker and the audience is essential for the whole development of the argument.

In this campaign, the speaker becomes trustworthy because of his character. The Brazilian public, for the most part, likes people who are simple, shy, weak, sympathetic

---

[7] This statement by Carlos Moreno was taken from an article about Garoto Bom Bril, obtained from the Internet. However, there was no date on the text. We believe it must have been made between 1986 and 1988.
[8] Excerpt from the text by Maria Elisa Vercesi de Albuquerque available at www.centrocultural. sp.gov.br.
, **The story of the replacement of Garoto Bombril in** http://www.abacaxi atomico.com.br /our-columnists/ sal/59.htm **Accessed 16/11/2014.**

and cordial.

People also feel passionate about the speech that deals with their emotions. When saying goodbye to the housewife in the 1981 campaign (quoted in this article), the Bom Bril boy confessed that he had lost his job because of "gossip" and because people didn't like his "effeminate" manner. The public's passion for his speech can be seen in the reaction of the listeners, who believed that the fact was real. When he returns to television later, to the delight of the people who didn't sympathize with another supposedly "unsympathetic" and "bossy" boy, he thanks them, "because jobs aren't easy these days". This resource, called *pathos* by Aristotle, makes use of emotional evidence that is used to persuade the audience.

In the opinion of Washington Olivetto, in an informal interview in 2000, "because he's very human, like his audience, he can grow old in the role, he doesn't need to be replaced. It has a lot of reality content, so it can acquire everyday characteristics".

2.3.1. The Bom Bril Boy on the back covers of magazines

From 1997 onwards, what had already been a great success on television moved on to printed magazines. The results of these campaigns were also so positive that, in 2000, the book "Soy contra capas de revista" - a commemorative collection of print advertisements - was launched during the International Book Biennial in Sao Paulo.

In this work, 24 of these magazine back covers were analyzed[10]. For each of them, the author of the campaign, Washington Olivetto, made comments, published in the book and transcribed below:

1- Good shine... Good in the kitchen and at the World Cup too - *May 1998. The atmosphere of the World Cup is starting to take hold of the country of soccer. Our character joins in with his experience as the world's only advertising star who has taken part in five World Cups: 78,82,86,90,94.*

2- Gel Gomes warns: always have these four elements in your kitchen. July 1998. Gil Gomes is one of Brazil's best-known police journalists. His voice and language are very well known to the public. On television, when he was launching the new Limpol Gel, Carlos Moreno was surprised by the journalist as he imitated him. At the same time, in magazines, Carlinhos played the character Gel Gomes.

3- Good shine. Every mommy loves this little guy. July 1998. Xuxa's 8-month pregnancy was competing with the World Cup for the attention of all Brazilians.

4- Women prefer Bom Bill. In other words: Bom Bril August 1998. On January 7, 1998, Monica Lewinsky denied her affair with US President Bill Clinton. On January 12th, the first evidence of the affair emerged: a tape. The case dragged on in the newspapers until June 30, when Monica Lewinsky handed a dress with sperm stains on it to prosecutor Starr. On August 6th, Monica gives evidence to the grand jury and confesses to having had sexual relations
"incomplete" several times with the president. At that point, we realized that Bom Bril could no longer refrain from discussing such a relevant issue. We went on television and

---

[10] All presented at the end of this article.

to the back pages of magazines to defend the sexual freedom of the American president.

5- *Clean Dja*. August 1998. The futurologist Walter Mercado says: "turn on dja" on television. An ad that had to be made dja, dja.

6- *My name is Bom Bril*. September 1998. In October, the unbearable electoral advertising schedule would begin again on Brazilian television. 45 days earlier, we had parodied one of the presidential candidates. Despite the parody, his vote was only 2.14% against 56.03% for the elected candidate Fernando Henrique Cardoso, which clearly demonstrates that our campaign is good for selling cleaning products. Thank God for that.

7- *Buy Bom Bril, auntie, buy it.* November 1998. Former W/Brasil trainee Luciano Huck creates the character Tiazinha on his show H , on the Bandeirantes network. The speed with which this ad was created and broadcast ended up unintentionally helping to turn the São Paulo phenomenon into a national one. But all the credit really goes to Tiazinha.

8- *Look at the Bombrileza!* February 1999. BomBrileza , inspired by Globeleza, created by Hans Donner in 1990 and, since then, the symbol of carnival at Globo.

9- *Nice promotion, Fernandinho.* April 1999. In the Bom Bril Quase de Graga promotion, Carlos Moreno was almost the president, almost the first lady...

10- *Make your cleaning wishes come true.* May 1999. A new woman is bewitching men on television and in the pages of Playboy. And the same character (dressed up!) continues to bewitch the women of Brazil.

11- *Good shine and cleanliness. Dating assumed.* August 1999. While TV presenter Luciano Huck and singer Ivete Sangalo publicly admit to dating, Carlos Moreno assumes his ability to represent even couples.

12- *Dirt and filth!* August 1999. It's not just Folha's Ratinho who's a hit on TV. Always in the know, the campaign couldn't have been unaware of the popular phenomenon that the other Ratinho has become.

13- *Good shine and cleanliness. This marriage works.* September 1999. TV presenter and model Adriane Galisteu stars in a flash wedding and divorce. As is the production of Bom Bril's print ads. In most cases, an ad is created, approved, photographed and produced in no more than 24 hours.

14- *Bom Bril top-notch cleaning.* October 1999. Milene Rodrigues, an embassy record holder, had already played ball with the W/Brasil team. She charmed everyone on the agenda. But she really charmed daddy Ronaldinho (Ronaldinho never played with the W/Brasil team).

15- *Good shine. He'll do anything for cleanliness.* October 1999. Many people who started collecting Bom Bril advertisements asked: "When is Silvio Santos coming?" He did.

16- *0 poor dirt!* October 1999. Gorete became one of the most successful comedians on TV. And we made humor out of humor. Poor competition.

17- *Don't echo the dirt.* October 1999. The brilliant Joao Gilberto complains about the echo at the inauguration of Credicard Hall, Sao Paulo's newest concert hall. The issue is echoed throughout the media and Bom Bril's communications.

18- *Good & Shiny. Sisters in shine and cleanliness.* October 1999. Brothers Sandy and Junior start selling records like Bom Bril. They deserve the quote.

19- *In the kitchen, no one has any more Ibope.* October 1999. Presenter Ana Maria Braga moves her audience from Record to Globo. She inspired this magazine ad. By the way, did you know that, before working in television, Ana Maria Braga was a very competent magazine professional, working in the commercial department of the publisher Abril?

20- *Dirt, get out of my face, get out.* November 1999. For a while now, some publicists have started dressing like pagoda dancers. Or is it the pagodeiros who have started dressing like some publicists? Well, never mind. In any case, advertising couldn't be unaware of the huge popular penetration of pagodeiros like Alexandre Pires, for example.

21- *Good shine. Powerful against dirt.* November 1999. After years, Brazil once again has a world boxing champion. Our super featherweight Popo. Our super-lighter Bom Bril didn't let it go.

22- *Without "Bombiril", I don't "garavo". I mean, I don't clean.* December 1999. Character inspired by the Brazilian comedian who created the most characters: Chico Anysio and his genius Alberto Roberto.

23- *With Bom Bril, dirt always loses.* March 2000. Rubinho Barrichello turned Brazil red. But we had to remember that the red of Bombril has been part of the country for a long, long time.

24- *It's not good for dirt to accumulate at home. Use Bom Bril.* March 2000. Nicea Pitta, ex-wife of the mayor of São Paulo, denounced her husband and created Pittagate. That's why Bom Bril is so careful with all these ads. We know the power of our target audience.

3. THE CLEAN ARGUMENT

In the ads, the Bom Bril boy lent his body to publicly credible personalities, thus establishing greater credibility for the written text and greater acceptability for the argument. The association of the word with the image is the most significant rhetorical resource common to all these advertisements published on the back covers of magazines from 1997 to 2000. The rhetorical value of the image of Xuxa, Ronaldinho and other public figures lies in the pictorial message's ability to implicitly raise an argument, which will be completed in the minds of those who see the image. The written sentence is completed in the person's mind by an implicit argument: the person also imagines themselves to be Xuxa, Ronaldinho, Gil Gomes; and, identifying with this character, they accept the message that Bom Bril is good, since it is preferred by these personalities they admire.

Ronaldinho's statement "Bom Bril...Bom de cozinha e de copa tambdm" is more convincing than that of any other person. If Gil Gomes warns, we should believe him. Xuxa, queen of the little ones, is also the mother who likes "Bom Bril". If futurologo Walter Mercado says "Ligue dja", people will call. So it's only fair to call Bom Bril if he's the one asking. And if Tiazinha asks, you should buy it. Even Silvio Santos said that Bom Bril is the one that "will do anything for cleanliness". And when Filo says: "O, poor dirt", it must be because Bom Bril "cleans first class" (just like Ronaldinho getting Milene pregnant). As Nicea Pitta, ex-wife of the mayor of Sao Paulo, says, "It's not good to accumulate dirt at home". In the kitchen, "no one has any Ibope anymore", says Ana Maria Braga. That's why Bom Bril only got the Oscar statuette for "1001 nominations in the cleaning category".

Analogies establish a relationship of similarity between two relationships linking two entities. It's not a question of similarity between the entities, but between the relationships that link each pair. The relationship between A and B is similar to the relationship between C and D. Its function is to clarify the second comparison term by the first.

We can recognize examples of analogies in advertisements. Just as Ronaldo is "good in the World Cup", Bom Bril is "good in the kitchen"; the product is adored by mothers and the "little ones" are adored by Xuxa; just as Bill Clinton was women's favorite, so was Bom Bril; just as the sorceress can make your wishes come true, Bom Bril products can do the same; Ana Maria has high ratings in the kitchen in the same way that the brand's products do; dirt suffers similar action to that of racing driver Barrichelo: he always loses; and just as it's not good to have a relationship with "dirt", it's not good to accumulate it at home either.

Comparison is considered a persuasive strategy because it allows the speaker to present the compared objects according to their preferences and persuasive intentions. Through this resource, the speaker induces the listener to accept his opinion. It consists of confronting two truths and concluding on the relationship between them. Pauliukonis (1996, p.48) states that "in order to know the relationship between two things, it is necessary to know the two parts beforehand", and that "comparisons are made through subjective circles and confrontation is the instrument that language uses to define individuality". Because it is subjective, comparison always tends to modify a pre-existing state of affairs and "lends itself much more to arguments in favor of the sender's reasoning than to objective information about the facts of reality", although it is a strategy used by the sender to abstract arguments capable of capturing the interlocutor's adherence to their thesis and leading them to an expected conclusion.

Analyzing the structure of comparisons in a discourse allows us to translate the argumentative intent present in the enunciations of a text, making us reflect on the order of preference of the enunciating subject and the strength of these arguments for capturing the interlocutor's adherence.

For example, a comparison is made between two situations: TV presenter and model Adriane Galisteu has a flash marriage and divorce, but the same will not happen between Bom Bril products and cleaning, as they will never separate. This comparison reinforces the value of the product, since, at the time, separation was not yet very well accepted by Brazilian housewives.

In October 1999, Joao Gilberto complained about the echo at the inauguration of Credicard Hall, Sao Paulo's newest concert hall. Taking advantage of this fact, the company launched another advertisement, making a comparison between this situation and saying that we can't give an echo to the dirt, the situation in our homes has to be different and, for that, we have to use the brand's products.

3.1. Bom Bril's rust-free language

Another important resource used in the Bom Bril campaign is the innovation of advertising language, introducing colloquialism, which favors the audience's adherence to the thesis, their communion with the speaker. In order to better persuade his audience, rhetorical figures are present in the texts.

Rhetorical figures play an important role in argumentation. According to Reboul (1998, p.114), "The figure is only rhetorical when it plays a persuasive role", and, "if the argument is the nail, the figure is the way to nail it".

A figure of speech is a stylistic resource that allows the enunciator to express himself in a different way than usual. Not all figures can be considered rhetorical; only those that play a persuasive role.

Perelman (1999, p.195) states that the figures could be grouped into three: of choice, of presence and of communion. Their objectives are, respectively, to impose or suggest a choice, to increase presence and to create or confirm communion with the audience through references to a common culture, tradition or past. Everything depends on the context in which the enunciative process takes place and the enunciator's objectives in the task of persuading the audience.

Figures of speech refer to the sound material of the speech and their persuasive power is due to the fact that they "facilitate attention and recall", as well as "establishing an apparent but incisive harmony, suggesting that if the sounds are similar it is not by chance. The harmony is proven by pleasure" (Reboul: *op.cit., p.* 118). The puns "bom bril/ bom Bill", "bombrileza", "topa tudo por limpeza" and "Popoderoso" illustrate the power of these figures.

Figures of speech concern the meaning of words or groups of words. They consist of the use of a term (or several) with a meaning that is unusual for it. According to Reboul *(idem, p.120)*, "the figure of speech plays a lexical role; not that it adds words to the lexicon, but that it enriches the meaning of words".

Metonymy brings about a relationship of contiguity between the substituted term and the substitute, and this can be observed in almost all the ads when analyzing the image. The consumer identifies the characters represented by the advertisement boy through metonymic features. The teeth, the bald head, the national team uniform identify Ronaldo; the position of the hands, Gil Gomes; the hair and the pregnant belly, Xuxa; the beard, the glasses, the austere physiognomy, Eneas; the whip and the mask, Tiazinha; the skin color, the dark body paint, Globeleza; the veil and the position of the hands, the Sorceress; the stick, the moustache and the hair, Ratinho; the smile and the microphone, Silvio Santos; the turban, make-up, clothing, the character Filomena played by Gorete; the guitar and the tongue sticking out, Joao Gilberto; the hair tied up, Louro Jose and the microphone, Ana Maria Braga; the suit and the color of the skin, Alexandre Pires; the boxing glove, the fighter Popo; the suit, scarf on the neck, net in the hair, the character Alberto Roberto; the red overalls and helmet, Rubinho Barrichelo.

The metaphor is also present in many advertisements when elements of meaning from a different field are applied to the world of cleaning products. In this way, the characteristic aspects of this field are transferred to domestic activities, adding new meanings and values. The term "copa", which would be a reference to the world soccer championship, takes on the meaning of the part of the house linked to the kitchen that will be cleaned with Bom Bril. The "little guy", who would be the child who accompanies Xuxa, becomes Bom Bril. The aunt, our mother's sister, becomes the character Tiazinha. The term "de primeira", referring to Milene's pregnancy which occurred during the first meeting between the couple, also acquires a new meaning in relation to cleanliness. Dirt also acquires a new meaning: it is no longer used in the connotative sense but in its original sense with Bom Bril.

Personification is also evident in the ads through the "courtship" between Bom Bril and Limpeza and the "marriage" that works out. Philo's expression "The poor thing" is also because "dirt" is not a human being for us to feel sorry for. "Bom & Bril" are not brothers like Sandy and Junior. It should always be Rubinho who loses, not dirt, because he's not a Formula 1 racer.

FINAL CONSIDERATIONS

In this article, we summarize some of the basic characteristics of Rhetoric as an art of persuasion in its traditional Greek form and in its more refined modern reformulation, which sees it as an art of argumentation.

Rhetoric in advertising was addressed, with the aim of showing that its study as an art of persuasion is not restricted to mere academic interest.

A number of rhetorical studies are currently being carried out on advertising texts, but they always deal with language resources (metaphor, hyperbole, ellipsis, allegory, metonymy, etc.) which are also adapted to images. In this work, in addition to analyzing the rhetorical figures that are essential to provoke passion for persuasive discourse, we have taken a further approach: we have used some concepts about Rhetoric presented by the philosophers Aristotle and Chaim Perelman to analyze the texts, emphasizing the importance of convincing an audience through argumentation.

According to Aristotle, we are convinced by the ethical appeal of the speaker who lends his credibility to the sale of the product and by the emotion that is provoked in us by the epidictic discourse whose main objective is to show, to exhibit its object and Chaim Perelman states that the receiver is convinced to buy the product by the choice of premises by the issuer. There is a communion that must be established between the audience and the speaker.

By analyzing examples of Bom Bril's advertising texts published on the back covers of magazines, we can justify the success of the campaign: the use of rhetorical resources and arguments are the most efficient means of convincing and persuading different audiences.

An argument is not necessarily a proof of truth. It is, above all, a linguistic resource designed to get the interlocutor to accept the points of view of the speaker. However, only those who have developed their argumentative skills will be able to convince others of the validity of their arguments.

If Bom Bril continued to have a specialized technician presenting only the characteristics and chemical elements of its products until today, it would be difficult to maintain contact with such a universal, varied audience.

Through the use of argumentative techniques and rhetorical resources, we can defend our representations of the world through the use of convincing words. Rhetoric can be an efficient sponge to remove the "rust" from words and worn-out arguments so that the rhetorical resources used in speeches can shine and attract consumers of our ideas.

REFERENCES:

ABREU, Antonio Suarez. **The Art of Argument. Managing Reason and Emotion.** 3.ed. Sao Paulo: Atelie Editorial, 2001.

ALBUQUERQUE, Maria Elisa V. de. **Garoto Brombril: a creative phenomenon advertising.** Revista D'Art, Sao Paulo, Centro Cultural Sao Paulo, p. 27-32, 1998.

ARISTOTELES **Arte Retorica e Arte Poetica**. Trad. Antonio Pinto de Carvalho. 16ª ed. Rio de Janeiro: Ediouro Publicagoes S.A. [19--?]

Rhetoric. 2nd edition, revised, Lisbon: Imprensa Nacional Casa da Moeda, 2005.

CUNHA, HELIA Coelho Mello Cunha "The Art of Persuasion" in **Argumentação Juridica**. Rio de Janeiro: Ed. Freitas Bastos, 2004.

MANOSSO, Radames. **Elements of Rhetoric** Available at www.radames.manosso.nom.br/retoricaAcesso 15/11/2014

MATOS, Rodrigo Cdsar de Andrade. "The Artifices of the Television Advertising Message for the Sustainability of the Bombril Brand - a Case Study". Federal University of Juiz de Fora, Faculty of Social Communication, 2007. Available at http://www.ufjf.br/facom/files/2013/04/ Rodrigo Cesar de AndradeMattos.pdf Accessed 16/11/2014.

O GAROTO BOMBRIL in http://www.wtennis. com.br/html/revistas/67/carlos.htmAccessed 15/11/2014

PAULIUKONIS, Maria Aparecida Lino. "Comparison and Argumentation. Two complementary notions". In SANTOS, Leonor Werneck dos (org.) **Discurso, coesao e argumentação**. Rio de Janeiro: Oficina do Autor, 1996, p. 48-56.

PERELMAN, Chaim & OLBRECHTS-TYTECA, Lucie. **Treatise on Argumentation - The New Rhetoric**. transl.Maria Ermantina Galvao Sao Paulo: Martins Fontes, 1999

REBOUL, Olivier. **Introduction to Rhetoric**. Sao Paulo: Martins Fontes, 1998.

Soy Contra Capas de Revistas / W/BRASIL.Sao Paulo: Negocio Editora, 2000

ANNEXES:
ADVERTISEMENTS[11]

[11]Soy Contra Capas de Revistas / W/BRASIL.Sao Paulo: Negocio Editora, 2000

BOM BRIL
QUASE DE GRAÇA
BONITA PROMOÇÃO, FERNANDINHO.

BOM BRIL
REALIZE SEUS DESEJOS DE LIMPEZA.

BOM BRIL
BOM BRIL E LIMPEZA. ESTE CASAMENTO DA CERTO.

BOM BRIL LIMPA DE PRIMEIRA

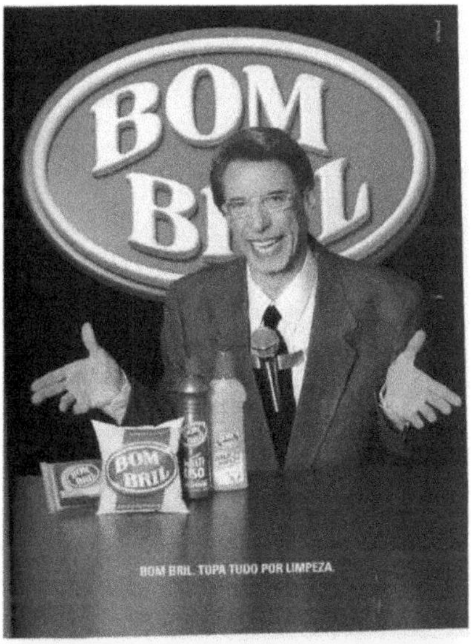
BOM BRIL
BOM BRIL. TOPA TUDO POR LIMPEZA.

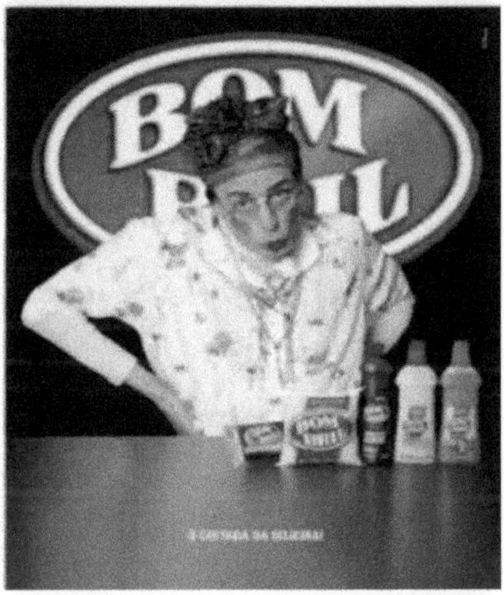
BOM BRIL

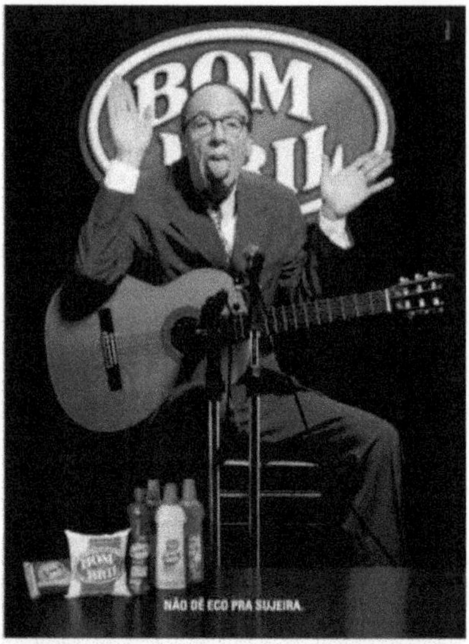
NÃO DÊ ECO PRA SUJEIRA.

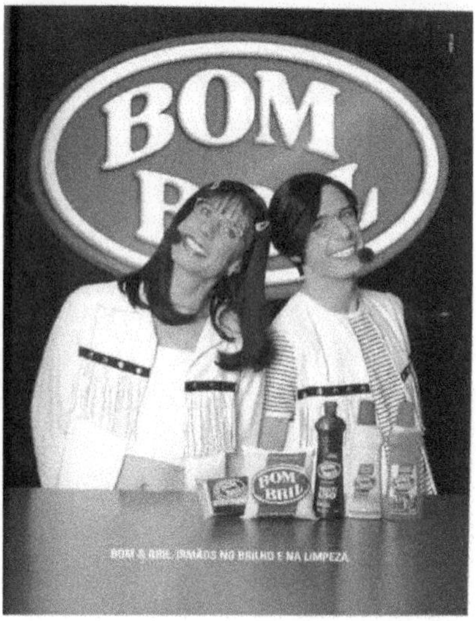
BOM & BRIL. IRMÃOS NO BRILHO E NA LIMPEZA.

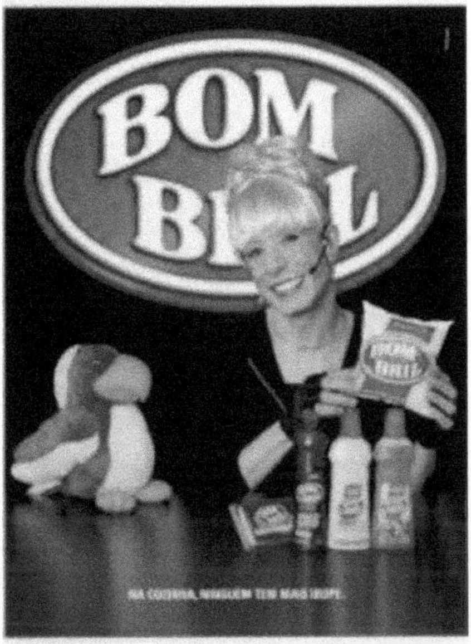
BOM

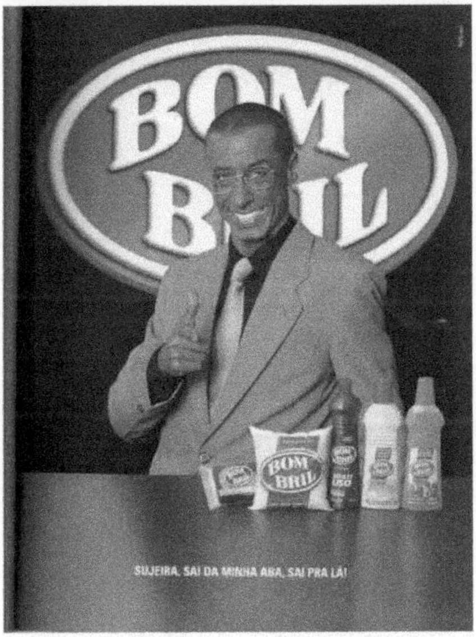
BOM
BOM BRIL
SUJEIRA, SAI DA MINHA ABA, SAI PRA LÁ!

BOM BRIL
BOM BRIL. POPÓDEROSO CONTRA A SUJEIRA.

BOM BRIL
SEM "BOM BIRIL", EU NÃO "GARAVO". DIGO, NÃO "LÍMPIO".

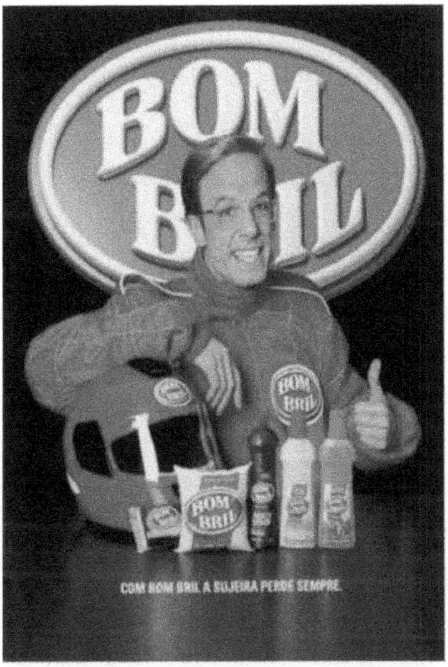
BOM
BRIL
COM BOM BRIL A SUJEIRA PERDE SEMPRE.

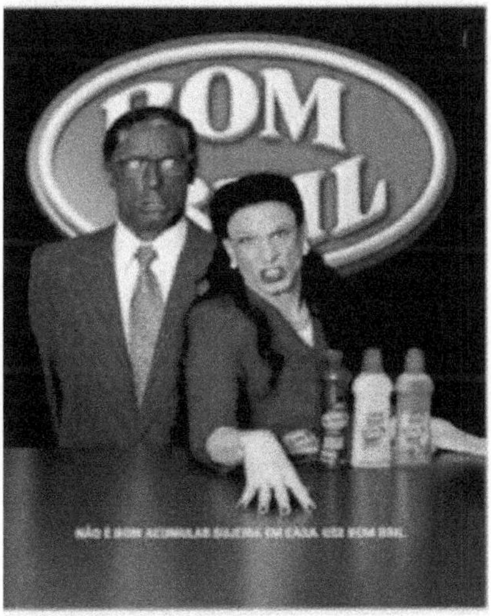

III-SOFISMS AT SCHOOL: EDUCATION PREVENTS MANIPULATION[12]

1. SOPHISTRY AND SOPHISTS

Some of the thinkers, orators and teachers of argumentation from Greece in the 5th century BC (and the beginning of the following century) are called sophists. They were characterized by Plato as imposters, shitters interested in rich young men, didactic merchants and athletes in verbal combat, purifiers of opinions, jugglers of arguments that were more truthful than true and more seductive than plausible. Sophistic arguments exist to this day. But what is sophistry?

Gustavo Bernardo[13] (2009) states:

By the 5th century, sophistry was the thesis defended by the sophists. At that time, sophists acted as teachers, teaching the children of noble families, and were prepared, like modern lawyers, to show how to argue for or against any opinion. Sophists followed an argument wherever it led them, without worrying about personal, moral, civic or religious considerations. Because of this practice of free thinking, perhaps too free, over time the term "sophistry" acquired a pejorative connotation, coming to mean an argument used to deceive rather than to clarify or arrive at the truth. Some philosophers say that "sophistry" is an argument with malice, that is, constructed with the conscious intention of deceiving the interlocutor, while "fallacy" would be an argument without malice, that is, constructed without the intention of deceiving, but misleading just the same. (...) It's important to study sophistry for two reasons: firstly, to realize when other people's arguments are trying to deceive us; and secondly, so that we don't commit sophistry in our own writing out of haste, laziness or ignorance.

The aim of this article is to make Brazilian school teachers aware, through some current examples, of the importance of studying sophistry so that students can use this knowledge to analyze other people's arguments and avoid being manipulated by today's "sophists". Knowing how manipulation occurs is fundamental to the formation of a citizen.

---

[12] Article produced on the oral communication entitled "Sophisms at school: education avoids manipulation", presented by the author during the XII LATIN AMERICAN CONGRESS OF HUMANITIES, held at UENF on October 14, 2016.
[13] Is a sophism a sophism? Available at http://www.revista.vestibular.uerj.br/ coluna/coluna.php? seqcoluna=25 Year 2, n. 4, 2009. Accessed on 20/11/2014

2. RHETORIC: PERSUASION OR MANIPULATION?

Persuading is not the same as manipulating. The big difference lies in the speaker's intention. The aim of persuasion is to provoke an audience's adherence to the speaker's thesis by appealing to rational and emotional factors. **Persuasion represents the** good use of Rhetoric. It occurs when the speaker's intention is to get an audience to adhere to a thesis not by imposing it, but by accepting it, since the objectives of the argument are clearly explained. The speaker uses the word rationally, encouraging the listener's critical spirit and autonomy.

Manipulation, on the other hand, represents the misuse of rhetoric, considered by some authors to be "black rhetoric". Manipulation occurs when ideas are imposed and the speaker tries to avoid the audience's reflection and freedom of decision by presenting his ideas in an implicit, confusing way, in order to prevent reflection and the listener's ability to evaluate. The manipulator tries to disregard the listener's individuality and freedom of decision; what matters is the achievement of their interests. When the intention is manipulation, rational factors are devalued and the speaker appeals to emotional adherence: the speech is based on fallacies and the main intention is to confuse the audience; there is manipulation whenever someone tries to control the knowledge of another, conditioning or altering their behavior.

White rhetoric tries to uncover the procedures of black rhetoric and is therefore critical, lucid and aware of the different forms and problems involved in communication, while black rhetoric corresponds to an illegitimate use of discourse, because it aims to deceive, mislead and manipulate the interlocutor. "Black rhetoric", as Barthes called it, is rhetoric that sets out to make conclusive, truthful and fair what it actually poses as a question[14]. Meyer (1993, p.46-51) states that "language: it serves the truth, but it is not enough to guarantee it by itself. It can cover up lies, it can seduce and convince, just as it can manipulate and deceive. If rhetoric is useful, it is because it allows men to exercise their critical sense and judgment in full awareness".

---

[14]MICHEL MEYER, *Questions of Rhetoric: Language, Reason and Education.* Lisbon, Edigoes 70, 1993, pp. 46-51.

3. MANIPULATION BY SOPHISTRY

Borges; Paiva and Tavares[15] (2016) state that there are two types of manipulation: affective and cognitive. Affective manipulation is centered on appealing to the recipient's emotions and feelings, while cognitive manipulation operates by falsifying the content of the speech.

According to the authors, the manipulation of affections occurs when:

Seduction by the person or demagogic seduction (ethos): seduction by resorting to (false) behavior and attitudes that can impress the audience. The typical demagogic speech is one that alters its message according to the audience in front of it. (...) Seduction by style: using figures of speech to escape the content of the speech and impress through form. Today, the idea of being clear, transparent and concise predominates. This idea is the hallmark of the *mass media,* even if sometimes the speeches are so concise that they distort the information. It's an example of the "style of clarity" as a form of seduction. (...) Aestheticization of the message: the use of art (artistic figures) in order to seduce. In advertising, for example, the use of public figures, film and television artists, etc. is common. (...) The use of fear: a situation of fear is created through the abusive use of authority, which ends up acting as a conditioner. The manipulation of children is a typical example of this. (...) Repetition of the message: words, ideas, sounds or images are repeated so that what initially seemed unacceptable no longer seems so. (...) Hypnosis and synchronization: based on the laws of classical conditioning, psychoanalytic studies and, above all, neurolinguistic programming. A relationship is built with the audience by synchronizing gestures, breathing rhythm, tone and rhythm of voice, and then moving on to vocabulary, ideas and concepts. At a certain point, the (almost) hypnotized person becomes unable to resist the message entering their mind. (...) Use of touch: physical contact or its suggestion can be used to increase adherence to the message.

And cognitive manipulation, according to the aforementioned authors, occurs when there is

Lying framing: lying about the facts or presenting the facts in a way that distorts them, taking the false for true or vice versa. (...) Abusive reframing: orienting the facts in such a way as to distort reality, inducing illusion. (...) Coercive framing (obligatory, there is no option): some facts are concealed, a situation is created in which a first message is accepted, which is nothing more than a trap to impose on the receiver the real message to which adherence is sought. Amalgamation: mixing the message with external elements, suggesting a link between the two (without providing any basis).

3.1. Sophistry through emotional manipulation:

When emotion is used in place of a logical, coherent argument, a sophism of

---

[15] BORGES, -ГсБё Pereira; PAIVA, Marta; TAVARES, Orlando. Argumentation and Philosophy in New Contexts. Philosophy, 11th grade. Porto Editora, 2016.

emotional appeal occurs. Appeals to emotion are efficient forms of manipulation, since all human beings are influenced in some way by emotion.

There are various sophistries in this field, which is why the teacher must present them to his students so that they understand these tactics and avoid being manipulated.

Let's take a look at some of them:

3.1.1. Appeal to authority

It occurs when there is an aestheticization of the message; even though the person selling the product is not qualified to give an expert opinion on the subject, it can be well done. accepted by the audience he wants to persuade because he is a public figure they like.

Figure 1: SEARA advertisement
Source:http://expressoanaliseecritica.blogspot.com.br/2014/11/analise-de-peca-publicitaria-seara.html Accessed: 29 Aug. 2016.

3.1.2. Appeal to fear

The argument presented is based solely on the fear that is instilled in the receiver of the message. The audience is induced to do physical activity by the fear they feel of becoming like the left side of the person shown in the ad.

Figure 2: Advertisement for the company Iniciativa Fitness
Source: http://www.dote.com.br/anuncio-escolha-seu-lado?page=2 Accessed: Aug. 29, 2016.

3.1.3. *Argumentum ad infinitum*

Regardless of whether a proposition is true or false, the repetition of certain statements can be effective in producing beliefs, which gradually become consolidated in the individual and turn into "truths". In the advertisement below, there is manipulation by repetition, as well as hypnosis and synchronization.

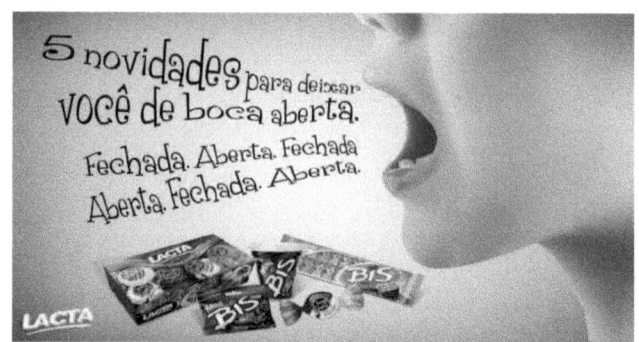

Figure 3: Lacta advertisement
Source: http://julianaportuguesfeevale.blogspot.com.br/2011/11/anuncio-da-lacta.htmlAcesso: Aug. 29, 2016.

3.2 Cognitive manipulation sophistry and abusive reframing

These are sophistries related to the manipulation of facts by a lying framework, which fail to effectively prove what they claim. Let's look at some of them:3.2.1 Omission of evidence

The author of the sophistry tries to justify the fact with false evidence, masking the truth.

"Fui levada à delegacia porque eu sou uma cidadã favelada. Meu carro foi rebocado, mas já amanhã (segunda-feira) mesmo vou tomar as providências para pegar de volta. Se eu quisesse ir embora, dava 10 reais para eles. São todos mortos de fome mesmo."
Tati Quebra-Barraco, a funkeira que sempre que é flagrada infringindo a lei se diz perseguida por ser "favelada", ofendendo os PMs que a pegaram dirigindo seu Citroën Picasso sem habilitação

VEJA 22/11/06

Source: Veja magazine. 22 Nov. 2006.

3.2.2 Appeal to tradition

The fundamental argument is "the older, the better". Translation was the only argument presented in the Bohemia beer ad to defend the idea that the product is good. It only appealed to tradition, with an attempt to manipulate it by framing it as a lie.

Figure 4: Bohemia.
Available at:<http://www.putasacada.com.br/wpcontent/uploads/2012/02/bohemia.jpg> .
Accessed on Aug. 26, 2016.

3.2.3. After the fact, and therefore because of it

It's the mistake of believing that because one event precedes another, the first must cause the second. This sophism is widely used today.

> "O frango que comemos está cheio de hormônios femininos. Por isso os homens que comem frango têm desvios em sua masculinidade."
>
> EVO MORALES, presidente da Bolívia, iluminando uma conferência sobre mudanças climáticas

Source: Veja Magazine, 17/12/2008

3.2.4. False analogy

Between the situations presented as similar, there are many more differences than similarities.

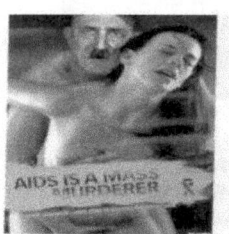

PUBLICIDADE

Hitler é pior que a Aids

Está gerando polêmica na Alemanha a imagem da nova campanha televisiva de prevenção à Aids. O público em geral e os médicos em particular estão a exigir que ela seja retirada do ar. Eis a peça publicitária: uma cena mal iluminada mostra um casal fazendo sexo. Aos poucos a cena vai clareando até que fica tudo visível. **O rosto masculino que surge é do ditador nazista Adolf Hitler, acompanhado dos dizeres: "A Aids é genocida."** O motivo dos protestos é que a associação de um criminoso a uma doença pode levar ao preconceito contra os portadores de HIV. Ou seja: nem a Aids é pior que Hitler.

Source: Revista Epoca. 09 jul.2008

3.2.5. Hasty generalization

There is a conclusion based on insufficient evidence, a judgment of everything in a given universe based on a small sample. This is the case where the exception is considered the rule.

Figure 5: Folha de Sao Paulo newspaper ad
Source: http://www.putasacada.com.br/folha-de-sp-wbrasil/Acesso Aug. 29, 2016

3.2.6 Statistical sophistry:

The news item on the front page of the newspaper O GLOBO in 2011 presents statistical data that leads the reader to believe the thesis being defended. However, if the context is analyzed, the sophistry is revealed:

Figure 6: Front page of O GLOBO newspaper
Source: http://emirlarangeira.blogspot.com.br/2011_11_01_archive.html.Acesso 21, Nov.11.2014

If we consider that, in 2011, there were 17 UPPs located in the area of 38 neighborhoods in Rio de Janeiro (most of them in the South Zone) in a universe of 160 neighborhoods in the capital, 90 in Sao Gongalo, 48 in Niteroi and 91 in Nova Iguagu, we can see that these data are misused to present a false reality, since, in these regions alone, we would have a total of 229 neighborhoods without UPPs.

3.2.7 Slippery slopes

It's an argument suggesting that if we allow something to happen, consequently something else will happen, with certainty or good probability, followed by something else, and so on down a "slippery slope", until we reach a clearly undesirable situation.

Let's look at this example of an argument put forward by President Lula, highlighting the extent to which consumers' decision to avoid shopping could worsen the country's financial situation: "Someone has to tell them [the consumer] that they're going to lose their jobs precisely because they don't buy. When they don't buy, industry doesn't produce, commerce doesn't sell and somewhere it's going to explode. And it's going to break out exactly in industrial production". (SEE-05/12/2008)

3.2.8 False dilemma

The writer offers a limited number of alternatives when, in fact, there are more.

In the example below, Archbishop Aloisio Lorscheider of Fortaleza told Veja magazine:

Figure 7: Dom Aloisio Lorscheider's statement
Source: Veja magazine. Sept. 2012

3.2.9 Irrelevant conclusion

An argument that claims to prove one thing actually leads to a different conclusion.

"O que a gente vê nesses casos é uma pessoa que sai armada de uma faca, agride, a ponto de levar essa pessoa à morte. É um delinquente que tem que ser tratado com a dureza da força policial. Não tem jeito. Isso não é um problema social."

Eduardo Paes
Prefeito do Rio de Janeiro

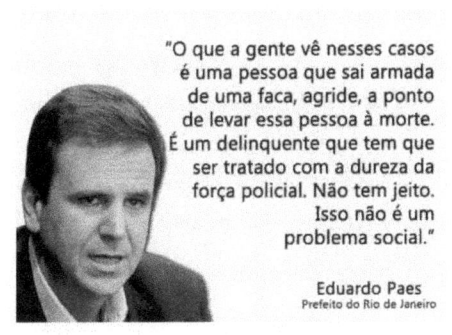

Figure 8: Eduardo Paes' statement
Source: Veja 21/05/2015

3.2.10 "Twisting the facts" sophistry

The evidence for the phenomenon being explained is biased, it's manipulation by amalgamation. An example of sophismatic propaganda is the Banco Itau campaign entitled "Itau without paper", broadcast on the internet and on TV. The bank induces customers to avoid using paper by showing a video of a baby laughing while doing so. By advocating saving paper, it's actually a strategy to reduce operating costs, since the bank can offer the same services while reducing its expenditure on paper.

Figure9: The "Itau paperless" campaign on the internet and TV.
Source:http://www.mobilizado.com.br/sms/campanha-bem-sucedida-do-itau-ganha-deployment-mobile Accessed Aug. 29, 2016

FINAL CONSIDERATIONS

The role of the school in preventing and combating manipulation is fundamental as it is the place where critical thinking develops. Manipulation is dangerous because it compromises an individual's autonomy and identity. The ability to recognize sophistry helps prevent manipulation, which is why studying this subject is essential.

By presenting and analyzing the various sophistries in advertising texts and current statements in newspapers, magazines, television and the internet, we illustrate the importance of this subject in reading classes in Brazilian schools. By tackling this subject, we believe that students will be able to develop a critical sense; an essential ability for them to be participating citizens in the pluralistic society in which we live.

REFERENCES:
ANDRADE, Tcвë Rogërio de Pinho. Fallacies or Sophisms. Available at http://jrparoge.blogspot.com.br/2011/11/falacias-ou-sofismas.html. Accessed Aug. 28, 2016.

Atheists.net. Stephen Downes' guide to logical fallacies Available at https://ateus.net/artigos/ceticismo/guia-de-falacias-logicas-do-stephen/. Accessed: Aug. 28, 2016.

BERNARDO, Gustavo. Is a sophism a sophism? Available at http://www.revista.vestibular.uerj.br/coluna/coluna.php?seq_coluna=25 Year 2, n. 4, 2009. Accessed on Aug. 28, 2016.
Restless Writing. 5ª ed. Belo Horizonte: Formato Editorial, 2000.

BORGES, Tcвë Pereira; PAIVA, Marta; TAVARES, Orlando. Argumentation and Philosophy in New Contexts. Philosophy, 11th grade. Porto Editora. Available at: https://www.portoeditora.pt/conteudos/emanuais/.../41018/.../ncon11_arg_e_fil.pptx Accessed Aug. 28, 2016.

MEYER, Michel, *Questions of Rhetoric: Language, Reason and Seduction,* Lisbon, Edigoes 70, 1993, pp. 46-51.

I want morebooks!

Buy your books fast and straightforward online - at one of world's fastest growing online book stores! Environmentally sound due to Print-on-Demand technologies.

Buy your books online at
www.morebooks.shop

Kaufen Sie Ihre Bücher schnell und unkompliziert online – auf einer der am schnellsten wachsenden Buchhandelsplattformen weltweit! Dank Print-On-Demand umwelt- und ressourcenschonend produziert.

Bücher schneller online kaufen
www.morebooks.shop

info@omniscriptum.com
www.omniscriptum.com

OMNIScriptum